AUSTRALIA IN COLOUR

AUSTRALIA IN COLOUR

by
ROBIN SMITH

LANSDOWNE PRESS
MELBOURNE

Lansdowne Press Pty Ltd
37 Little Bourke Street Melbourne 3000

First printed 1963
Reprinted 1963, 1965, 1966, 1969, 1970
This edition reprinted 1971

THIS BOOK WAS PLANNED AND DESIGNED IN AUSTRALIA
BY LANSDOWNE PRESS, MELBOURNE. TYPE WAS SET
BY DUDLEY E. KING LINOTYPERS PTY. LTD., MELBOURNE.
COLOUR NEGATIVES WERE MADE BY TOKYO SCANNER CO.
LTD. TOKYO. IT WAS PRINTED AND BOUND BY TOPPAN
PRINTING CO. LTD. TOKYO, JAPAN.

INTRODUCTION

THAT THIS was a land of promise, beauty, colour and individual character seemed borne in my first glimpse of Australia. All that I had read and heard of the splendour of Sydney Harbour became inadequate as I watched from the bow of the liner on that balmy January morning in 1959. The cliffs flanking the Gap and North Head and, beyond, the generously bush-covered harbour headlands, thrusting out between small bays and beaches, were faithfully reflected by the oily calm. Farther ahead were lazing merchantmen and yachts; beyond these again, great buildings standing high in the morning sun and a glimpse of the unmistakable hump-backed bridge. Somewhere over to the right in a grove of wattles and gums, as if by arrangement, some kookaburras throated their distinctive greeting. This could only be Australia.

My sentiments were not shared by those Europeans who first visited Australia's shores, or the Asiatic explorers who are thought to have come to Australia centuries earlier. For hundreds of years after Ptolemy's legendary *Terra Incognita* was found actually to exist, the continent was neglected and despised. Jansz, Hartog, Carstensz, Houtman, de Vlamingh and other Dutch navigators who charted the coasts of New Holland in the Seventeenth Century discouraged interest in the new territory by their unfavourable reports. The findings of the British buccaneer, William Dampier, on his visits to the west coast in 1688 and 1699 aroused interest but no enthusiasm from the British. Even after Captain Cook's discovery, charting and formal claim to possession of the eastern part of the continent in the name of the British Crown, the British Government was not prepared to consider colonization of Australia. In fact, had it not been for the loss of the greater part of the American colonies in the War of Independence, it is doubtful if European colonization would have begun as early as it did.

Forced to find alternative accommodation for her overflowing jails, Britain substituted the undeveloped territory of New South Wales for the plantations of Virginia and Maryland. The First Fleet carrying 1,500 persons, 800 of whom were deportees, reached Botany Bay on January 18 1788, and a week later transferred to Port Jackson, there to begin the settlement of Sydney. Although those first settlers found themselves, against their will, in a new land half way across the world, it offered them a new horizon of freedom and opportunity.

My introduction to Australia was a memorable one; in fact it has been one of my most unforgettable moments in this new land. To me Australia was a new land only in a sense. Being born of proud Australian parents, I knew enough about it to experience, on many occasions, that eerie feeling of having been here before.

In five visits in four years, and in the course of travelling some 100,000 miles within its 12,000 mile coastline in an assortment of vehicles, boats, aircraft and on horseback, I have become increasingly aware that this is a land of bewildering size and diversity. I realize now, that if I were to travel about it at a similar rate for many more years, I would still not have seen all; but I believe I know the character of the land and its people. For both, I have great admiration and respect.

Can you visualize a land more than eleven times as big as Texas, bigger, in fact, than the U.S.A. below the 48th parallel, or nearly as big as Europe excluding Russia? Picture an island 2,000 miles from head to heel and 2,500 miles across its girth. It is the only continent occupied by a single nation and has never been invaded or torn by civil war.

This is no ordinary colossus. It is the oldest continent on earth, cradle of the Australian Aborigines, who, themselves, are many thousands of years older than any other human race, and who, today, in the twentieth century, are only just emerging from the Stone Age. It has been host also to a vast range of unique and distinctive plant and animal life which has contributed greatly to the character of Australia.

In America there are odd examples of the marsupials, those unusual animals which are equipped with a built-in cot and perambulator for their young. Here, in Australia, over one hundred and fifty kinds have survived from the dream-like ages of antiquity. Among them are the Tasmanian tiger (rarest of them all); kangaroos and koalas, almost synonymous with Australia itself, which have endeared themselves and this country to many people in all parts of the world.

There are unique egg-laying mammals represented by the echidna and the fur-coated platypus, the latter being an animal oddity without equal. The platypus, an odd combination of bird, mammal and reptile, is almost as old genetically as animal life itself.

The kookaburra, which has the vernacular name of laughing jackass, the lyre bird (prince of mimics), the giant wedge-tailed eagle, birds of paradise and the strange brolga, or native companion, whose ceremonial dances have been incorporated in many aboriginal dances and legends, have lent individuality to Australia too. So have frilled lizards and goannas, and termites that build their blade-like hill homes always facing north and south.

The koala, kangaroo, kookaburra and platypus have all made strong contributions to the character of Australia, but none as much as the gum trees or eucalypts. Few Australian landscapes are complete without them. In common with so much of Australia's flora and fauna, the eucalypts are living representatives of the very distant past—millions of years old. Like the marsupials, almost without exception these trees have survived in Australia only. Among them are the tallest hardwoods in the world: the mountain ash trees of Victoria. Before bushfires and milling gangs took their toll, specimens of these trees more than 300 feet high were recorded—the undisputed monarchs of the aboreal kingdom.

Wattles, or acacias, six hundred species of them, also add to the picture of Australia, with their colourful flowers and forms. But for sheer colour, the myriads of seasonal wildflowers that engulf the landscape in every state following spring and summer rains are without equal. Western Australia has six thousand different ones, and every state has a host which are peculiar to it, and of which they are justly proud.

Australia, with the exception of insular Tasmania, lies evenly balanced above the scimitar sweep of the Great Australian Bight, carved by the restless Southern Ocean. To the north the fretwork edge of the continent is washed by the monsoonal Timor and Coral Seas. To the west the land thrusts aggressively into the Indian Ocean and to the east its boomerang-shaped backbone points towards New Zealand, its nearest neighbour, 1,200 miles away. Within this irregular perimeter are the six states and two territories, large and small, that comprise the Commonwealth.

In preparing the contents of this book, the publishers and I have purposely avoided the pictures which show the impact that Australians have made on their country, the tremendous industrial development, ever expanding and ever present in the lives of the urban population. This is a book of the Australian countryside and coastline. Those who accompany me on this pictorial journey will see that this is not an endless expanse of semi-desert with stockmen riding the boundary fence, but one of infinite change. You will glimpse orderly green paddocks saturated with sheep, and seemingly limitless expanses of sienna-coloured landscape, palled in frightening stillness, stretched out beneath a tremendous sky. You will view mountains bathed in such a furnace-red light they look like heaps of near-molten metal; sheets of water thundering in headlong flight through forests of limitless greens; steel-grey cliffs locked in their endless struggle with the sea, and quiet havens crowded with boats. You will also see sunburnt waterless gorges and placid landscapes with meandering rivers, chilling snowcapes, deep-blue tropical bays, boldly modelled giant gum-trees, great sweeping, smooth stretches of sand, and mountains steeped in pastel-blue haze. All of these are Australia.

R. S.

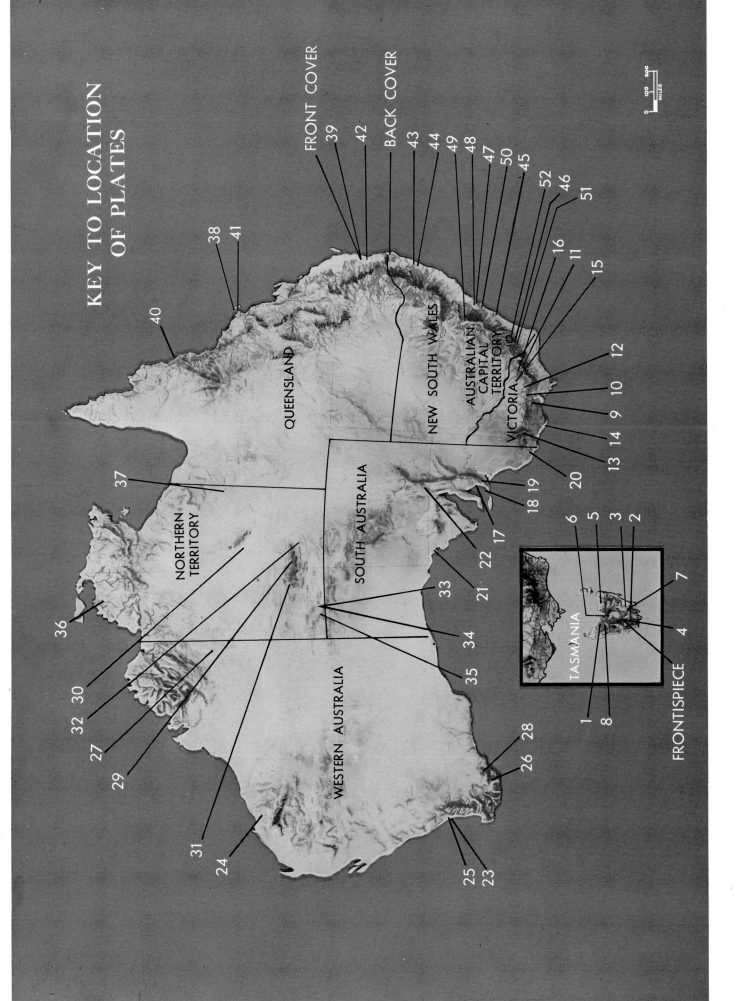

KEY TO LOCATION OF PLATES

ON THE southern edge of the fertile coastal belt of north Tasmania there is a densely-forested mountain barrier, about 4,000 feet high, called the Great Western Tiers. From the sea, it looks like an almost unbroken wall, but actually some parts of this fault-escarpment are higher, or detached from the main line, like Quamby Bluff, Black Bluff, St. Valentine's Peak, and the subject of this picture, Mount Roland.

Beyond lies the Central Plateau, like a table-top sloping gently to the south, and clustered with lakes. The Western Tiers have a special claim to fame, as the home of a creature thought by many scientists to be the oldest form of animal life in existence; this is the straight-backed shrimp, known from fossils to have lived in the seas of the Carboniferous Age, but surviving to this day only in the icy pools of Tasmania's mountains.

The placid and beautiful Sheffield countryside shown in this picture is close to the villages of West Kentish and Wilmot, on the way to Waldheim Chalet in the Cradle Mountain–Lake St. Clair National Park. Here rich-green rolling pastures give way to the misty purple and blue of the forest-clad mountains, which cannot fail to appeal to even the most blasé tourist.

PLATE 1
Mount Roland, Tasmania.

BEYOND Eagle Hawk Neck, which narrowly saves Tasman Peninsula from being an island, there is a coast of fierce and rugged splendour. This is an area where much of the land has sunk beneath the ocean, and where the great waters strike savagely at the remnants of the highlands now reduced to sea-level, sculpturing them into roughly hewn coves, bold headlands with overhanging cliffs, sea-caves and blowholes. This massive promontory is on the south-eastern side of Eagle Hawk Neck, very close to the Blowhole, the Devil's Kitchen and the well-known Tasman Arch cave. Farther south, the hexagonal columns of black dolerite at Cape Raoul, Cape Pillar and Tasman Island rise sheer to 600 feet above the water.

On the shores of one of the quieter bays of this peninsula, the major penal settlement of Port Arthur was established in 1830, and operated until 1877. By then, a large proportion of the 67,000 convicts transported to Tasmania, or Van Diemen's Land, as it was then called, had passed through its grim walls. The ruins of this settlement, nowadays visited by thousands of people, remain as a reminder of the darkest days in Australia's colonial history.

PLATE 2
Tasman Peninsula coast, Tasmania.

LOOKING at the symmetrical arches of Richmond Bridge and the peaceful countryside mirrored in the tranquil waters of Coal River, it is hard—and painful—to realize that this was once the scene of such bitter suffering. For this bridge, Australia's oldest, built between September 1823 and January 1825 with convict labour, witnessed the hatred and anguish of desperate men, and the pitiless cruelty of their guards. Testimony to the care and skill with which it was constructed is evident in its perfect present-day condition; it is now a vital link in the modern motor-road carrying speeding cars and heavily laden trucks.

Another fine convict-built bridge spans the Macquarie River at Ross, on the Midland Highway near the centre of the island; and a third superlative example of this type of bridge, which crossed the South Esk River at Perth, near Launceston, was swept away in a devastating flood in 1929.

Victoria and New South Wales each have stone bridges, still in use, which were built by convict gangs at about the same time. The Lennox Bridge, in New South Wales, was completed about a year after Richmond Bridge.

PLATE 3
Richmond Bridge, Tasmania.

TASMANIA is the only State in Australia with an overall generous and reliable rainfall; the predominating westerly winds drop their moisture on the mountainous central plateau where the peaks reach over 5,000 feet above sea-level, and there it is conveniently stored in the many old glacial lakes.

On this moisture depend three widely differing aspects of the Tasmanian scene.

It makes possible the intensive cultivation of the green and gracious farmlands and orchards on the scimitar-shaped belt of fertile country running from the north-west to the south-east of the island.

It provides a great hydro-electric potential, for this State is the only one in which all electricity is generated from water-power. The low cost of production has attracted many important industries, such as the aluminium and ferro-alloy plants at Bell Bay, the newsprint mills at Boyer, paper and board mills at Burnie, zinc and fertilizer works at Hobart, and a carbide plant on the d'Entrecasteaux Channel.

The great Tasmanian rain-forests are also dependent on this abundant moisture. They provide not only a valuable industry, with about fifty different timbers of commercial importance, but an unending store of beauty and interest. Leatherwoods, celery-top pines, sassafras, tree-ferns—all are lovely in their natural setting; and the great forest areas, still largely uninhabited, and in a few remote parts of the south-west, still unexplored, are strongholds of native birds and animals. The shy Tasmanian devil, a carnivarous marsupial, and the nearly extinct marsupial wolf are among the most interesting creatures found there.

This boldly green rain-forest scene was recorded in the Mount Field National Park.

PLATE 4
Stream and forest, Mount Field, Tasmania.

THE deep and rich russet and chocolate-coloured soils of northern Tasmania are among the finest mixed-farming lands of Australia. The generous rainfall produces wheat, oats and barley, and heavy crops of vegetables used mainly for frozen foodstuffs; it also lends itself to the production of beef, mutton and wool, as well as intensive dairying which contributes to a chocolate-manufacturing industry.

This photograph, taken near Scottsdale, thirty-nine miles east of Launceston, shows an area where bulbs are grown for export to many parts of the world. The orderly paddocks, rich green in pasture and young crops, rust-red in fallow, and golden with ripening cereals, spread a colourful patchwork over the quietly rolling countryside at the foot of the pine plantations—a part of the only softwood forest in the island.

Farther south, this restful landscape changes to the rugged country that culminates in the peaks of Legges Tor and Ben Lomond, both over 5,000 feet high, and both within the boundaries of a national park which is particularly popular with skiing enthusiasts in winter.

PLATE 5
Scottsdale cultivation scene, Tasmania.

SIDE by side with her wonderful rugged mountain scenery, Tasmania has stretches of countryside that show an almost English serenity. The oast-houses and hop-fields of the Derwent, the picturesque orchards near New Norfolk, the hawthorn hedgerows and freestone walls and buildings of the centre and north, the patchwork of paddocks, deciduous old-world trees and soft-green pastures all contribute to this effect.

But for the scattered gums in the left middle distance of this emerald-green landscape near Westbury, about twenty-five miles west of Launceston, it could be a European scene. Quamby Bluff, in the background, is one of the most dominant features of the Great Western Tiers, beyond which are cradled the numerous glacial lakes of the Central Plateau, including the Great Lake, Tasmania's largest.

Above the banks of the South Esk River, a few miles nearer Launceston, stands what is perhaps Australia's most interesting and best-preserved historic building. This is Entally House, built in 1820 as the manor-house of the village of Hadspen. In 1948, it was bought by the government, and carefully restored and refurnished with authentic early colonial furniture by the Tasmanian Scenery Preservation Board.

PLATE 6
Westbury landscape, Tasmania.

NOWHERE is the historic past better preserved than in Hobart, capital of Tasmania and second-oldest city in Australia. Although the population has grown to 120,000, and modern glass-walled office buildings and motels, super-highways and a massive concrete bridge have sprung up, an old-world charm remains.

From the 130-year-old shipyards facing Wrest Point, through historic Battery Point to the line of old freestone warehouses along Salamanca Place, there are constant reminders of the turbulent and romantic past. Even in the heart of the city mellowed Georgian houses and stores more than a hundred years old stand cheek by jowl with their trim, modern counterparts. It is perhaps around Constitution and Victoria docks, where this picture was taken, that Hobart's character remains most in evidence; here the masts, spars and canvas-carrying booms against the stoutly-constructed buildings of the harbour bring a constant reminder of the city's early days.

Hobart was founded in 1804, on the banks of the Derwent River, under the 4,165-foot peak of Mt. Wellington. From its unrivalled deep-water port, great quantities of primary products are exported—wool, zinc, paper, timber, chocolate, and the fine apples for which the island is famous. The docks are not only among the cleanest in the world, but also among the most picturesque. Fishing-boats, luxury yachts, rusty coasters, business-bent ocean freighters and sleek liners all berth here within a stone's throw of the city's centre, continuing to reflect and preserve Hobart's briny soul.

PLATE 7
Hobart, Tasmania.

EVEN in Tasmania, where spectacular mountain landscapes are so commonplace that they almost cease to be arresting, this view of Dove Lake and the twin peaks of Cradle Mountain and Little Horn is perhaps supreme. It lies at the northern end of the spacious Cradle Mountain—Lake St. Clair National Park, in the heart of the State, and it owes its existence to the Ice Age.

During that period, Tasmania's central tableland was heavily eroded by huge sheets of ice which, when they receded, left mountains of harder rock high above the general level of the countryside, and hundreds of gouged-out depressions which became lakes.

Cradle Mountain and Little Horn, as seen in this picture from the north, form an interesting cirque. From here, two glaciers carved out several lakes, but left the serrated columns of the dolerite heights looking like great coxcombs, reaching to 5,069 feet. Dove Lake, because it lies in a sheltered basin almost surrounded by hills, is placid and colourful—often a rich blue, sometimes nearly black. Surrounding it, and reaching up the mountainsides, is a variety of beech and pine trees; and in summer the slopes are splashed with colour from the blossoms of the flowering shrubs and plants.

Until quite recently, the inaccessibility of this area prevented all but a few prospectors, trappers, or hardy adventurers from reaching it. A rough track from Wilmot in the north provided the first reasonable means of access. Then, an Austrian built an accommodation house of axe-hewn pine-logs, in the style of his homeland. He called it Waldheim—a home in the forest—and it is still in use. The original track has now been improved to a good motor-road, and much of the 525 square-miles of the national park has well-marked walking-tracks and huts, maintained by competent rangers and bushmen.

PLATE 8
Cradle Mountain and Dove Lake, Tasmania.

CULTURE and commerce have been strangely but most successfully wed in Melbourne, Victoria's capital city at the head of Port Phillip Bay. In spite of its development into a metropolis of 2,000,000 people, Melbourne has preserved great dignity and serenity. Slender spires and fine old buildings merge with the modern colossi of business, and the tree-lined boulevards and river-banks hint of the Botanic Gardens and the parklands for which the city is known.

A stroll beneath the cool, green trees of Collins Street will unfold much of this dual character. You will walk past the ornamental facades of the great commercial buildings of an earlier period, with the occasional modern giant towering up between them; you will pass exclusive little salons, mellowed churches, pavement-cafes gay with umbrellas; if you turn into Exhibition Street you will go by theatres, car showrooms and restaurants, and a fine place to end a tour of the city is the National Gallery in Swanston Street, with its world-famous art collection.

Melbourne is a fascinating, sophisticated and beautiful city. Something of its varied charm is captured in this view along the tranquil Yarra River.

PLATE 9
Melbourne, Victoria.

CRADLED between high forested hills about forty miles north-east of Melbourne is Maroondah Reservoir. The Melbourne and Metropolitan Board of Works, which controls this city water-supply, has made a feature of the area around the dam by laying down extensive lawns, gardens, shrubberies, and many deciduous trees.

As a result, Maroondah has become one of the most popular picnic resorts for a day's outing from Melbourne. In autumn, frosts paint a leafy picture in surprisingly strong reds, yellows and golds, as shown in this photograph.

Two miles back along the Maroondah Highway is the attractive township of Healesville, with its famous Sir Colin McKenzie Wild Life Sanctuary. Here many species of Australian birds and animals, including the unique platypus, can be seen in near-natural conditions.

PLATE 10
Maroondah, Victoria.

WHEN winter comes, the Australian Alps take on a new beauty in the snow that lies deeply upon them. The slopes that were gay with wildflowers and birds are now strangely quiet; the cattle that foraged among the alpine plants have gone to lower pastures, and only the hardy snow-gums remain here and there, clinging tenaciously to life—and sometimes losing it, like these on Mount Hotham.

Skiers alone delight in the snowy capes which the mountains wear; from many of the slopes in the south-eastern corner of the continent, from Mount Kosciusko's 7,316-foot bulk in southern New South Wales to Mount Donna Buang close to Melbourne, comes the winter song—the harsh whisper of speeding skis.

Mount Hotham, Swindler's Valley which plunges away from it, and nearby Mount Feathertop are in the heart of Victoria's skiing grounds.

PLATE 11
Snow-gums on Mount Hotham, Victoria.

ABOUT 100 miles north of Melbourne, in an area of heavily forested mountain-country, is a wonderful pleasure resort with a very practical purpose. A huge earth dam has been built across a valley, forming the artificial lake of Eildon with its 320-mile shore-line. This dam not only provides hydro-electricity and an extensive irrigation and flood-control system for the Goulburn Valley, but an ideal holiday spot with modern motels and well-equipped camping grounds. Its waters are stocked with trout and the voracious redfin, and its popularity as a boating and fishing resort can be gauged from this view of Boat Harbour.

Some of the statistics of the Eildon scheme are impressive. Its capacity of 2,750,000 acre-feet of water makes it six times greater in volume than Sydney Harbour. The Goulburn irrigation system is Australia's greatest project of its kind so far; provision is made for supplying water to 1,250,000 acres through 2,300 miles of channels. Agricultural, pastoral, dairy and horticultural products worth £20,000,000 annually are expected to be grown on the areas supplied by it.

PLATE 12
Eildon, Victoria.

THE Grampians mountains of Western Victoria are unequalled in their own style of rugged beauty. Although their highest peak, Mount William, is only 3,829 feet high, their steepness and isolation make them look much higher than they are. Their discoverer, Major Sir Thomas Mitchell, was deceived into believing them "of stupendous height", probably because for a considerable time he had been travelling over featureless flat country. Impressed by their resemblance to the Grampians of his native Scotland, he gave them the same name.

From a distance, the ranges contrast strongly with the predominant colouring of the plains from which they rise. First they appear as a vague blue outline above the raw and burnt-siennas whose only relief is the dull green of the scattered, shaggy eucalypts; then, as one approaches, they become intensely blue and purple—an exciting foil when seen apparently floating above the sea of golden-ripe wheat rippling before the north-west wind over the plains of the Wimmera.

Only from really close do the ranges reveal themselves in all the splendour of their wild configuration and varied colouring. Massive headlands, deep fissures and precipitous scarps of white, red, purple, brown and grey sandstone, and thin bands of shale stand out against the blue and grey-green of the forest. In the springtime comes a bounty of wildflowers—nearly a hundred varieties of terrestrial orchids are among the seven hundred odd species of plant-life found there. A wildflower exhibition at Hall's Gap each spring attracts streams of people from Melbourne, some 180 miles away to the east.

The Balconies, on Mount Victory, is the subject of this picture.

PLATE 13
Grampians, Victoria.

AMONG the cliffs of the coast near Port Campbell in western Victoria, are the most dramatic forms found anywhere along Australia's 12,000-mile coastline. Composed of loosely consolidated beds of soft clay, sand and limestone, they have been deeply eroded by wind and sea. Deep-tongued coves and far-reaching, thundering blowholes have been gouged out from the softer cliffs, between headlands of harder materials, some of which have been cut off from the mainland. Many of these islets have taken strange shapes, from grotesquely formed blocks to needle-sharp spires, as they disintegrate; a particularly impressive line of these residuals is known as "The Twelve Apostles".

The intense colour of the ocean, usually Chinese-blue or turquoise, sets off to perfection the amber, russet, ochre and gold of the cliffs that rise sheer for over 200 feet from the water.

The gorge illustrated was named Loch Ard after a ship which was wrecked there in 1878, with the loss of all but one crew member and one passenger. Those two owed their lives to the luck of being washed into this indentation, which has a small beach at its head. It is one of the few breaks in mile upon mile of high, unscalable cliffs.

Port Campbell, a fishing village and summer holiday resort, is 151 miles from Melbourne.

PLATE 14
Loch Ard Gorge, Victoria.

AUSTRALIA'S reputation as an agricultural and pastoral country is second to none. Few primary industries are not represented on the impressive production list, for as well as being the world's leading wool-producer, Australia exports enormous quantities of cereals, meat, dairy-products, sugar and fruit.

Except for the gold-rush era of the 1850s, nearly all industry was related to rural products until well into this century. Now, although highly industrialized rural production averages only about 20 per cent. of the gross national effort, 80 per cent. of Australia's export income is still of rural origin.

Once simply a way of life, farming has now become a highly competitive and specialized business as well. Constant research and skilful farm practice have resulted in lush pastures and magnificent beef cattle such as these becoming more the rule than the exception. This photograph, taken near Whitfield in Victoria, conveys an im-pression of peace and prosperity as well as showing the pastoral beauty of the Australian countryside.

PLATE 15
Cattle on pasture at Whitfield, Victoria.

IN THE Australian Alps, just over 200 miles north of Melbourne, is one of Victoria's most spectacular peaks. This is the 5,645-foot Mount Buffalo, sitting on its isolated granite plateau of about sixteen square-miles in extent, in the national park which bears its name. Headquarters for visitors is a spacious hotel called The Chalet, 4,400 feet up the mountainside, above Bent's Lookout with its sweeping panoramic views of Mount Feathertop, Mount Bogong and Mount Hotham, across the enchanting Bright Valley thousands of feet below.

Summer brings holiday crowds to drive, walk and ride among the weather-sculptured boulders and outcrops that jut through masses of wildflowers between the snow-gums; and in winter the slopes invite skiers and tobogganers.

This view shows part of the road leading to the summit, which is called The Horn. The 800-foot sheer walls of the gorge, almost immediately below the Chalet and Bent's Lookout, form one of the mountain's most striking features.

PLATE 16
Mount Buffalo, Victoria.

ADELAIDE was fortunate in having the services of a qualified surveyor, Colonel William Light (South Australia's first Surveyor-General), when the site and the layout of the city were decided on in 1836.

Against opposition from the small population which had landed at Glenelg with Governor Hindmarsh a few months earlier, Light chose a site on the banks of the Torrens River, midway between the Mount Lofty Ranges and the long sandy beaches of the St. Vincent Gulf, and decided on the admirable layout of the city. Adelaide has developed roughly according to his prescribed pattern, with the business area, principal public buildings etc. and North Adelaide across Lake Torrens, contained in the Adelaide Square-Mile. Surrounding this, and separating it from the residential areas, is a 1,700-acre green-belt of gardens, parklands and recreation grounds.

Today, the wide streets and squares are flanked by many tall buildings of modern design. But, a few minutes walk from the progressive and prosperous city, one may stroll through wide gardens, under a canopy of trees, or watch the pleasure boats and swans on the still waters of Lake Torrens. A few miles to the south, the Mount Lofty Ranges rise steeply from the plain, and cool streams tumble through deep ravines in the tree-studded slopes where farm animals graze.

This view of Adelaide from the north looks past St. Peter's Cathedral, over the cricket-oval and tree-lined Lake Torrens to the centre of the city, and the Mount Lofty Ranges in the background.

PLATE 17
Adelaide, South Australia.

SOUTH of Adelaide, past the suburb of Glenelg which was the landing place of South Australia's first settlers, through the picturesque vineyard landscapes of Reynella, and over the canal-like river of Onkaparinga (aboriginal for "fishing-place") is the bay of Yankalilla. It lies beside the almond orchards of Noarlunga and the pasture lands of Aldinga, on the western side of the peninsula which runs down to Cape Jervis and Kangaroo Island.

The scenery of Yankalilla Bay varies from gentle beaches to rugged cliffs backed by formidable hills. The line of Norfolk Island pines gives a touch of added beauty to this lonely but appealing coastal scene.

PLATE 18
Yankalilla Bay, South Australia.

LESS THAN 200 years ago, a few fat-tailed sheep from the Cape of Good Hope and a few Bengal sheep were brought to Australia to help feed the early settlers; today, this country, with a sheep population of 150,000,000 (about one-sixth of the world's total) is the major wool producer and exporter in the world. The initial credit for this achievement goes to John Macarthur, an army officer who in 1793 imported Spanish merinos with the idea of breeding for wool production rather than for meat. In 1807, he sold Australian wool in London for 10/4 a pound, and in 1827, a bale sent to London fetched one of the highest prices ever paid for wool. And, from the three to four pounds a head of those days, merino stud-masters of today have, through careful breeding, produced sheep which average nine to ten pounds a head.

Sheep-farming is by far Australia's most important rural industry, and her biggest single export-earner, bringing wealth to this continent from the far ends of the earth. More than nine-tenths of the wool produced in Australia is exported, providing about a third of the world's wool supply and more than half the world's merino fleece. Lamb, mutton and sheep-skins are also important products of this great industry, for Australia makes a big contribution to the food and clothing supplies of many countries.

Sheep are reared on country varying in carrying capacity between ten sheep to the acre and one to 100 acres. Even in areas where the annual rainfall is only seven to eight inches, sheep are grazed on the plains and slopes and tablelands, and the districts with better rainfall or irrigation are used for fat-lamb production. In New South Wales is the world's biggest merino-sheep farm, covering 240,000 acres, grazing 70,000 sheep, yielding a wool-clip of approximately 700,000 pounds.

Shearing is now done almost entirely by machine; the old hand-shears, like their picturesque users, have become memories of the past. But this picture endures—the quiet pasture-lands dotted with the sheep that carry so large a part of Australia's prosperity on their backs.

PLATE 19
Sheep in South Australian pastures.

A CHAIN of old volcanic craters, extending from western Victoria to the south-east corner of South Australia, achieves its most remarkable form in the Mount Gambier. This cone rises steeply for about 600 feet on the southern fringe of the city which is named after it. Within the main crater lie four small lakes—Browne Lake, Leg of Mutton Lake, Valley Lake, and—most beautiful of all—the Blue Lake.

Although quite strongly coloured all the year round, it is during the summer that this lake becomes the intense azure-blue that gives it its name. It is thought to be fed by underground streams coming from the mountains of western Victoria, and even the 100,000 gallons an hour drawn from it as the source of the city's water-supply, seems to make little difference in its level.

It was here that the well-known poet, Adam Lindsay Gordon, made his reckless jump on horseback over the boundary-fence of the lake on to a narrow ledge some 300 feet above the water.

The almost incredible colour of the Blue Lake, the steep confining walls of the old crater, are shown in this picture.

PLATE 20
Blue Lake, Mount Gambier, South Australia.

AMONG Australia's most interesting physiographical areas is the huge ancient sea-bed, known as the Nullarbor Plain, lying at the head of the Great Australian Bight. Its name is derived from the Latin words *null* (no) and *arbor* (tree), and, indeed, few trees other than saltbush and bluebush grow there. But its monotony is only skin-deep, for beneath the rather flat and featureless surface lies a maze of caverns and blowholes, some of them immense. There are no creeks or watercourses, and no evidence that any have ever existed there; all the ten to fifteen inches of rain that falls annually in the south percolates through the caves which have been dissolved by it from the porous limestone throughout the ages. The aborigines believed that a giant serpent had its home in these underground galleries, and that the dust-storms that blow on the plain were caused by the angry lashing of its tail.

The road runs through only some twenty miles of the fringe of the plain, but the railway crosses about 330 miles of it, in the longest straight stretch of line in the world. Travellers who have seen the pale skies stretching from side to side of the dust-veiled horizon, can find them changed, on calm days after rain, to an astonishingly vivid blue above the tawny land.

Where the plain meets the sea, the shore is quite dramatic and colourful in parts, as this picture of the coast near Streaky Bay shows. For much of the 1,000-mile sweep of the Bight there is a heavily serrated escarpment of two to three hundred feet in height. The ocean hereabouts has yielded some of the biggest sharks and other game-fish ever caught.

PLATE 21
Streaky Bay, on the Great Australian Bight.

THE RUGGED and colourful Flinders Ranges of South Australia have inspired many artists and photographers. Ever-increasing numbers of tourists and holiday-makers are visiting the area, particularly in spring when rain brings a blaze of red from the blossoms of the native hops.

Matthew Flinders, after whom these mountains were named, first sighted them in 1802. They are a continuation of the Mount Lofty Ranges which run from near Adelaide to the head of the Spencer Gulf; from there, they stretch northwards for another 200 miles, between the salt-pans of Lake Frome in the east and Lake Torrens in the west, growing higher and more rugged until they reach the Wilpena area; then they diminish again as they run on towards the place where they are finally lost beneath the desert sands of the north.

Considering the aridity of the region, there is a surprising amount of vegetation. Tea-trees, casuarinas and mallee grow here, as well as the beautiful and hardy cypress-pines, which give a parklike look to the mountain slopes, and the giant Flinders gums which the artist Hans Heysen painted with so much success. These gums always follow the creek courses, and are found nowhere else. But there is a constant struggle for existence between falls of rain, and many, like the cypress-pine shown in this picture, succumb.

PLATE 22
Flinders Ranges, South Australia.

PERTH, the capital of the vast State of Western Australia, is like a rare jewel in a gracious setting. It is flanked by the brilliant white beaches of the Indian Ocean and the gently rolling Darling Ranges, lapped by the broad and somnolent Swan River, and crowned with a 1,000-acre park of bushland overlooking the city. The climate is as magnificent as the location, for the average of eight sun-drenched hours a day makes it Australia's sunniest capital.

The friendliness and hospitality of its people, so genuine and spontaneous that it is unconsciously expressed, is known beyond the shores of this continent. Life is more leisurely than in the eastern cities, and everywhere there is evidence of strong civic pride. Given the opportunity, most of Perth's 425,000 inhabitants would be glad to show you the city's fine buildings, its historic landmarks, the broad reaches of the river populated by yachts, the open-air music bowl, the beautiful university, the Narrows bridge, the Kwinana Freeway leading to Fremantle and King's Park, the pride of Perth, on Mount Eliza. Here, in the spring, may be seen a sight of rare beauty—the natural bushland aflame with colour, when the profusion of wildflowers is matched by the flowering shrubs and trees above them. Among these blossoms, many of which would grace the finest garden, is the unique kangaroo-paw, the State's floral emblem. An open-air restaurant gives its patrons a superb view of the city, with the Swan River at its feet.

PLATE 23
Perth, Western Australia.

IN THE remote north of Western Australia, too far from any of the big cities and regular tourist routes for most travellers, lies some of the most colourful semi-desert country on the continent. Broome, Derby, Marble Bar and Wittenoom are little more than names on the map to most people, and the Carr Boyd Ranges go unadmired, though they are the match of many of their well-known counterparts.

The pyramid landscape shown in this picture, taken not far from Roebourne on the way to Wittenoom in the Hamersley Range, is such a place. It is stark, almost cruel-looking; but the colours are exciting. The land-forms, with their crumbling heaps of rock and the pyramid shapes where blocks of land are being worn from the plateaux, suggest erosion over millions of years; everywhere is the look and the atmosphere of heat and of great age.

PLATE 24
Pyramid landscape, Western Australia.

UNTIL the Dutch navigator and explorer, Willem de Vlamingh, discovered the black swan in 1697 on his journey up the tidal estuary of what is now called the Swan River, only the white swans of Europe were known to the world. Now, in parks and gardens throughout the globe, the Australian black swan adds the grace and beauty of its presence.

Although these birds look jet-black from a distance, they are actually not quite black, and there is some white on the wings; the bright red bill is in striking contrast to the dark plumage. Always regal in posture and movement on land or water, in the air they are magnificent, with their purposeful and confident flight in a steady V-formation. The aboriginal name for them, "Koonawarra", suits their flute-like calls.

Although their numbers have been reduced since European settlement, they are in no danger of extinction. Western Australians honoured the black swan by selecting it as their State emblem, and using its form on many of their stamps in pre-Federation days.

This picture was taken not far from the Swan River, at Lake Monger, Perth.

PLATE 25
Black swans at Lake Monger, Perth.

ABOUT twenty miles north of Albany, in the far south of Western Australia, a mountain range lifts abruptly from the level plains. The native name, Porongorup, sounds like the haunting chant of a didgeridoo—the native wind-instrument. Though only eight miles in length and about two in width, this range is quite spectacular, for in places the 2,000-foot-high granite peaks have been rent into blocks and slabs so sharp-edged and regular that they look as though they had been cut with a knife. Some of these walls, like Castle Rock, tower hundreds of feet above the forested mountains at their base; and these, in turn, look down upon the plain far below, where sheep and cattle graze on the surrounding farmlands, and apples, oats and barley are grown.

PLATE 26
Castle Rock, Porongorup, Western Australia.

THE Northern Territory, Queensland, and Western Australia each have cattle stations which are among the biggest in the world. These huge properties, which sprawl across the semi-arid hinterland which the Australian authoress, Mrs. Aeneas Gunn, named the Never Never, carry incredible numbers of cattle—up to 140,000 calves are branded annually on one station which employs a staff of about 125.

Aboriginal stockmen make a major contribution to the beef industry in the far north. These happy, good-natured men, in their picturesque outfits of colourful shirts, tight-fitting jodhpurs, riding-boots and broad-brimmed hats, obviously enjoy their work with the herds; able horsemen and instinctively good bushmen, they handle the mustering, branding, drafting of cattle with skill and confidence.

Pictured here is a group of native stockmen cattle-droving near Rose's Well on Mabel Downs station, in the Hall's Creek region of Western Australia. Dramatic thunder-clouds, such as these shown here, often belie their promise and provide little more than localized showers. The annual rainfall in the northern cattle country is only about ten to fifteen inches, and stock must depend almost entirely on water from artesian and sub-artesian bores.

PLATE 27
Aboriginal stockmen droving near Hall's Creek, Western Australia.

IN THE south-west corner of Australia is the land of Yilgarnia, which shares with the Musgrave Range of Central Australia the distinction of being the oldest part of this ancient continent. It is also one of the oldest land-surfaces on the face of our planet, for it came into being about 1,500 million years ago, before there was any form of life, even in the sea.

The great forests of jarrah, karri and tingle-tingle, the hills near Albany, the Porongorup and the Stirling Ranges are all in this area. Like the Porongorups, the Stirlings rise abruptly from the surrounding plains; but they run the full length of the horizon from east to west, and their spectacular peaks are much higher. The sheer-faced head of Bluff Knoll, shown here, is 3,640 feet high—the second highest mountain in Western Australia.

In the spring, a carpet of wildflowers adds a riot of fresh colour to the smouldering tints of an already colourful landscape — the brilliance of their young blossoms vivid against the aged earth.

PLATE 28
Bluff Knoll, Stirling Ranges, Western Australia.

RUNNING east and west of Alice Springs, the town which legend and history have established as a place of adventure and hard living, are the Macdonnell Ranges. Their reputation as mountains of fantastic beauty and colouring has spread beyond the shores of Australia, and they are now undoubtedly one of Australia's greatest tourist attractions.

Although these ranges, lying in almost parallel ridges for a length of about 200 miles, are near the geographical centre of Australia, they are quite accessible. Since the war, a sealed highway has extended 1,000 miles southwards from Darwin, and near Tennant Creek it is joined by the Barkly Highway; from Adelaide, another thousand miles to the south, come a road and a railway-line. Plane routes converge from north and south, and, from the oasis junction of Alice Springs, a road runs to the Glen Helen tourist lodge in the western heart of the Macdonnells, and to nearby Palm Valley; yet another road runs east to a tourist lodge in the Ross River area.

The ranges have a general elevation of 1,000 to 1,500 feet above the surrounding countryside, with a few peaks yet higher. About a thousand million years ago, they were probably 15,000 feet above sea-level.

Although these exceedingly hard quartzite mountains have been reduced to their present size by erosion, they are still wild and rugged. Here and there, deep gorges have been cut from north to south by rivers which have since dwindled into oblivion. Standley Chasm, illustrated here, is one of these gorges, and, although its walls rise sheer for over 200 feet, they are a mere twenty to thirty feet apart. To see this chasm during the few minutes when the midday sun streams directly across its walls is to witness a miracle of colour that can never be forgotten.

PLATE 29
Standley Chasm, Northern Territory.

IN STARTLING relief to the montony of the plains between Darwin and Alice Springs, is this curious concentration of rounded granite boulders covering several square-miles of the country through which the Stuart Highway passes. They vary in size from about a foot to over a hundred feet in circumference; some of them are balanced precariously on top of one another, and all are a rich golden brown, as though through long tanning in the hot sunshine. They are known as the Devil's Marbles, and they are strewn across the quartz-gravel plain as though it were indeed the Devil's playground.

These are the last remnants of the mountains that once existed there. Granite, in spite of its hardness, often weathers unevenly, resulting in the roundness of old rocks in this type of country; it also accounts for the "rocking-stones"—so rounded and so finely balanced that they can be rocked by hand, in spite of their immense size and weight.

PLATE 30
The Devil's Marbles, Northern Territory.

TO watch the sun's rays spread over Mount Sonder, in the western Macdonnell Ranges, is to witness a pageant of changing colours; turn away for a few minutes, and on looking again you will find the hues magically altered. As if this were not enough, the steep upper faces of the mountain reflect colours different from its base, above which it often seems to float.

This is the place which, more than any other, was painted with such success by Albert Namatjira, the full-blooded Aranda aborigine who achieved world-wide distinction as a water-colour artist. Until his death in 1959, he used his remarkable skill in recording the bold colours and perspectives of his native land. Others of the Aranda tribe are following in his footsteps.

Mount Sonder is but one of the many outstanding features within a few miles of Glen Helen, eighty miles west of Alice Springs. The Ormiston and Glen Helen gorges, through which the Finke River sometimes flows in frightening volume, Mount Giles and the strange wall-formations are all of absorbing interest and fantastic colouring. So is Palm Valley, a short distance to the south.

PLATE 31
Mount Sonder, Northern Territory.

WHEREVER trees grow in Australia there are eucalypts. From east to west, north to south, seashore to mountain-top, bog-land to desert, will be found one or more of the five hundred species of gums.

This magnificent specimen, dwarfing the man who stands at its foot, is a ghost-gum growing in the Ross River area, east of Alice Springs. Superb in colour and form, this tree lords it over all others there, able not only to live, but to thrive, in an environment where only the strongest may survive.

Ghost-gums have figured prominently in the works of many Australian painters, especially those of the Aranda school which developed at Hermannsburg Aboriginal Mission Station, west of Alice Springs. The water-colour work of these aborigines, of whom the late Albert Namatjira is the best known, has made an impact on the art of Australia and has received recognition throughout the world.

PLATE 32
Ghost-gums, Central Australia.

NEARLY three hundred road-miles south-west of Alice Springs is a magnet that draws tourists from all parts of the world—this planet's greatest monolith, Ayers Rock. Its massive bulk—nearly six miles in circumference and more than 1,000 feet in height—rises from a plain of drifting sand, spinifex-grass and mulga.

From about 150 miles away it becomes visible as a low purple mound; seen at closer quarters, it is bewildering, from the absence of anything in sight to indicate its scale. Through countless ages, the erosion of wind and water run-off has worn smooth its vertical strata, and hollowed out some of its flanks, leaving great steep buttresses between the fissures. From the summit of the rock a hardy climber may view the tors of Mount Olga, Mount Connor, and the vast sea of semi-desert on all sides.

PLATE 33
Ayers Rock, Northern Territory.

ULURU, as the aborigines call Ayers Rock, and the ritual rock-hole upon it, is a place of great importance to them. The name is derived from the word, "Ugulu", which, appropriately, means sacred and permanent. Every feature of the rock—strange 200-foot-long slab separated from the side for most of its length by a four-foot-wide gap; the numerous caves, some with aboriginal drawings; the water-holes, shelters and bluffs—each one of these has some particular significance to the aborigines.

To them, one of the most important parts is the source of Maggie Springs, or Mutidjula, the most permanent water-hole around the base of the rock. This photograph looks into the sacred water-python place above the springs, which legend says is the dwelling-place of the great Uluru snake. Should the Uluritdja people come to Mutidjula and find it dry, they would call out to the great snake, who, when disturbed, would disgorge water, which flowed down to fill the pool again.

A lot of the rock's catchment flows into the twin ravines above Maggie Springs, and there is always enough water to sustain these trees in the eastern fork as well as several pools between there and the one at ground-level. The rich red colour shown here is typical of the rock, but, like Mount Olga and Mount Sonder, its shade varies greatly according to the time of day and the distance from which it is seen. But at all times it is weirdly impressive, not only because of its immense size and amazing colour, but also through its unique atmosphere —like the ruins of some great temple of a lost and forgotten civilization.

PLATE 34
Maggie Springs, Ayers Rock, Northern Territory.

ON THE horizon to the west of Ayers Rock is Mount Olga, surely one of the most breath-takingly strange and colourful sights in the world. Unlike Ayers Rock, it is not a single stone, but a rough circle of enormous rounded granite monoliths, reaching 1,500 feet above the plain. The aborigines call it Katajutta, which means "Many Heads". Each is a smooth, jointless dome with sheer walls, and each is separated from its neighbours by chasms. Some, like the Pungalung Gorge, have water in them and are so big that they look like a canyon; others are surprisingly narrow fissures.

Because moisture is held here long after the surrounding country-side is desert-dry, there is a surprising variety of plant and animal life. Dingoes, wallabies, foxes, and land-shells are found.

Mount Olga is seen at its superb best when the last rays of the setting sun have turned its rock-faces to the glowing red of near-molten metal in a furnace.

PLATE 35
Mount Olga, Northern Territory.

A LANDSCAPE of extra-terrestrial fantasy is located just south of Darwin in the Northern Territory, where towering, concrete-hard blades with deeply serrated crests are spread over the plain. Similar ones are found on the Cape York Peninsula, but they are smaller than these, whose grey slabs have given the name of Cemetery Plain to the place where they are found.

They are called magnetic ant-hills—a double misnomer, for they are not magnetic, although they invariably point north and south, and the creatures which live in them are not ants, but termites. No scientific explanation has been made for their north-south alignment, but it is thought to be a device for gathering the greatest amount of heat from the rising and setting sun, and the least amount at midday when they are edge-on—a unique form of natural thermostatic control. They are built of peat-like earth mixed with saliva. Living-quarters are near the outer walls, and grass food-chambers in the interior.

PLATE 36
Magnetic ant-hills, Northern Territory.

NO PART of this continent is more "Australian" than the Outback —that vast open hinterland which is virtually as it was a hundred, a thousand, or a million years ago. It seems to symbolize the challenge presented to the pioneers by its endless space, heat and lack of water— as well as the opportunity, equality and freedom for which Australians have shown themselves ready to fight and die.

The fact that Australia is the most urbanized country in the world, with over seventy per cent. of the population living in the towns and cities, presents a strange paradox; for many of its inhabitants still like to think that the typical Australian is a tall, lean stockman, and that the typical Australian scene is the wide open spaces of the Never Never.

Such a scene is illustrated in this picture of the border-country between Queensland and the Northern Territory, where cattle stations of almost inconceivable size are found. Alexandria Downs Station, of which this country is a part, sprawls across 7,250,000 acres of the Barkly Tableland; it is the world's largest cattle station.

In spite of the emptiness, there is a certain austere beauty in the unbroken horizons under wide skies.

PLATE 37
Barkly Tableland, Northern Territory-Queensland border.

THE NORTHERNMOST landmark of the Whitsunday Group is Hayman, an island which has become a byword in the romantic tropic-isle holiday world. Although it appears as a mere dot on the map, a short distance off the Queensland coast near Proserpine, 600 miles north of Brisbane, it has made a far-reaching impact on the Australian tourist industry; for no longer does a holiday on a remote island involve living in discomfort for the privilege of visiting it. When Hayman was developed as a tourist resort, nothing was spared to make it a place for a delightful holiday.

It is a steep, heavily forested island of red granite, less than four square-miles in area, and shaped like a horseshoe. The half-mile-wide flat on which the buildings stand faces volcanic Hook Island and the other Whitsunday Islands to the south. Looking down from the hill behind the settlement, one cannot help being impressed by the beauty of the scene: fringing the long sweep of the coral bay are the separate modern units in which visitors are housed and the central block of air-conditioned dining-room, offices, lounges and restaurant built around a swimming-pool—all half hidden by palms, gay tropical trees, and bougainvillae. Beyond these are sleek-hulled catamarans, island outrigger canoes, and sailing-craft riding on a sapphire sea. Yet farther beyond are the high peaks of other islands, and less than an hour's run away is the Great Barrier Reef.

PLATE 38
Hayman Island, Queensland.

THRUSTING their sharp heads high above the exotic forests and native bushlands of the coastal plain fifty miles north of Brisbane are the Glasshouse Mountains. They are a group of ancient trachyte volcanic cores, which have been left standing long after their surrounding cones of softer material have been weathered away.

Captain Cook, whose attention they caught while he was in Moreton Bay in 1770, named them because of the wet, glistening rock of their summits, which reminded him of the glasshouses in his native Whitby in England. There are ten major peaks, ranging in height from 750 to 1,823 feet. Each member of the group has a resounding aboriginal name—Tibrogargan, Ngungun, Tunbubudla, Coonowrin; Beerwah is the highest.

This area, in addition to its striking mountain scenery, cultivates tobacco and is renowned for the pineapples grown on farms cut from the bush. There are also extensive pine-forests, and on the summit of one of the mountains is an important fire lookout-post to safeguard these trees.

PLATE 39
Glasshouse Mountains, Queensland.

MORE than half the State of Queensland lies within the tropics—a fact that affects much of the industry on the moist coastal belt east of the Great Dividing Range, which runs the entire length of the State.

The growing of sugar-cane is the most important feature, and the State's major agricultural industry. Some 8,000 farmers, with an average of sixty acres each, produce about 1,400,000 tons of sugar, worth £65,000,000, annually. Australians, who are the world's greatest sugar-eaters, consume about half of this, the rest being exported.

The fresh green of the young cane-crops, covering mile after mile of the gently rolling country and flats along the coastal belt, with intermittent breaks of terra-cotta fallow ground, creates a distinctive landscape. Heavily forested mountains on the landward side form a constant backdrop to this scene.

During the harvesting season, beginning in June and running for six months, roaring fires light the night skies or shroud the sunshine with smoke; for the cane must be burnt before cutting. The blackened figures of the cane-cutters and the tiny locomotives drawing long lines of trucks almost hidden under the loads of cane they carry to the mills, complete this picture of the tropical north.

The canefields illustrated here are near Cairns, the major city of the far north, which is a popular tourist centre as well as a port for the thriving sugar, mining, dairying and agricultural industries of the district and hinterland.

PLATE 40
Canefields at Cairns, Queensland.

LIKE Hayman Island, South Molle is one of the Whitsunday Group discovered by Captain Cook on his voyage of exploration in the Endeavour, nearly 200 years ago. Whitsunday Island and Whitsunday Passage he named because of the date of his arrival there; but Hayman, Molle and Hook are the names of some of his faithful crew-members. The whole area is still as Cook found it, so one can still experience a feeling of remoteness and adventure, although civilization is now a mere fifty miles away.

South Molle settlement has been built on the shore of a beautiful bay facing North Molle, Hook and Hayman Islands; like them, it is renowned as a holiday-resort with an atmosphere of informality with comfort. Only a little distance away, and reached by short excursions, is the Great Barrier Reef, which has been justly called the eighth wonder of the world.

This, the world's largest coral deposit, stretches 1,250 miles, from the coast of New Guinea to the Tropic of Capricorn, and covers 80,000 square-miles. These figures, though interesting, are un-important in comparison with the reef itself—the living reef, with its bewildering variation of form and colour, its exquisite corals and its prolific and brilliant fish.

PLATE 41
South Molle Island, Queensland.

CAPITAL of the huge State of Queensland, covering nearly a quarter of the Australian continent, is Brisbane, in the far southeast corner. Like the State it serves, it is big and roomy; for its population of 621,000, the metropolitan area of 474 square-miles is exceptionally large.

It is by far the most important commercial and industrial area in the State; many engineering, textile, metal and timber industries are centred there, as well as fruit and meat canning and the processing of dairy products. Its port is one of the busiest in the country.

Because of the warm climate and generous rainfall, Brisbane is gay with tropical flowers and shrubs; many of the avenued streets and gardens are alive with the colours of poinciana, jacaranda, silky oak and wheel-of-fire trees. In the shops and markets stalls are filled with tropical fruits and vegetables.

Not far south of Brisbane lies a famous twenty miles of Pacific shore stretching from Southport to the New South Wales border, and known as the Gold Coast. The beach resorts grouped under this collective name—Southport, Surfers' Paradise, Broadbeach, Burleigh, Kirra, Palm Beach, Currumbin, Miami, Greenmount and Coolangatta—have enjoyed a meteoric rise to popularity. Today they form a holiday city of about 34,000 inhabitants, with a large floating population.

PLATE 42
Brisbane, Queensland.

BEHIND the numerous almost privately individual bays near Coffs Harbour, is a fascinating tropical characteristic of the area. Fold upon fold of the steep, boldly sculptured hillsides are swathed in the huge green elliptical leaves of banana-trees; often, too, they are brightly splashed with the blue of thousands of plastic bags drawn over the ripening heads of fruit.

This is one of the greatest banana-growing districts in Australia; in common with the volcanic soils of the Tweed Valley farther north, it is rich enough for the greedy roots. Great quantities of the fruit are freighted to Sydney, 375 miles away, and to other cities of the south.

Coffs Harbour is also the greatest timber port in the country, with a very large wharf, built for timber-handling, running out from "Jetty Town".

Most of the many people who go to Coffs Harbour however, are more interested in the sunshine, golf, bathing and surf-riding, water-skiing, boating and the excellent fishing which the district provides. Coffs Harbour is also the gateway to the lovely Bellinger Valley, to Dorrigo National Park, and to other places within an easy day's drive.

PLATE 43
Coffs Harbour, New South Wales.

IT WOULD be hard to find landscapes of more surpassing tranquil beauty than those along parts of the Bellinger Valley. After their careless, headlong flight from the forested slopes of the Dorrigo Plateau, the waters of the Bellinger River are resting so placidly that they can mirror the parklike banks flanking their meandering course. As remote as other worlds are the dramatic, bizarre and exciting scenes of the inland with its wild colours, and the tension-packed streets of the great cities; here there is no struggle for survival; contentment and plenty, a harmony of scenery and atmosphere, flow through this landscape like the lazy river itself.

PLATE 44
Bellinger River landscape, New South Wales.

THE beaches of New South Wales have become more famous, perhaps, than those of any other State, though each State can truthfully boast in superlatives. The fact that Australians have established and re-broken many world records in swimming is no accident, for almost every Australian who lives within reach of the sea spends a good deal of time in it—for pleasure, even if not in the pursuit of style and form.

Unlike many of the beaches on American and Mediterranean coasts, the 12,000-mile shoreline which decks Australia like a scalloped necklace of platinum and gold, is open for everyone to enjoy—in fact, if not invariably by law; for, although there are a few properties with ownership right to the water's edge which were sold freehold in the early days, nobody has erected fences on a private beach, and nobody has been prosecuted for trespassing. Australia's coasts are truly free.

Swimming, surfing, sunbathing, boating, fishing—or just enjoying the tang of the sea air and the rhythm of the waves—all this is very much a part of Australian living.

The beach at Gerringong, New South Wales, is the subject of this picture.

PLATE 45
Beach at Gerringong, New South Wales.

THIS humble little township high in the Australian Alps has a special claim to be noted in the history of skiing, for it was here that the world's second-oldest ski club was formed.

In 1860 or thereabouts, soon after the first ski club was established in Norway, a Norwegian miner, reputed to be related to Amundsen of Arctic and Antarctic fame, was living in Kiandra, then a town of some 10,000 fortune-bent inhabitants. With some of the other miners, whom he had taught to ski, he formed the Kiandra Ski Club.

Today, skiing has about 60,000 active disciples in Australia; at Thredbo and Kosciusko, huge sums of money are being invested by companies who believe that skiing will soon become one of the major sports of the country. Thredbo, in fact, already has the appearance of a Tyrolean alpine village—but set in gum trees!

Many people find it hard to believe that this land, known for its hot sunshine and burning deserts, has real snow-country as well. It is certainly true that many Australians have never seen snow; but Tasmania, Victoria and New South Wales have snowfields so vast that they would more than cover Switzerland, and many of Australia's mountains provide long runs over smooth slopes or through country lightly timbered in beautiful snow-gums.

PLATE 46
Kiandra, New South Wales.

PLATE 47
Sydney, New South Wales.

BUILT around the 183-mile foreshores of Port Jackson, in a setting which has been admired and envied by people from every nation, is Sydney, oldest and largest city of the Australian Commonwealth.

Since its miserable inception as a penal colony in 1788, it has developed into one of the world's great cities—vigorous, purposeful, beautiful. To it come ships with the merchandise of the East, the Americas, Europe; and migrants speaking many tongues, to add their culture and the skill of their trades to a land which is assimilating the knowledge of several thousand years in its first two centuries of settlement. From it go vessels heavy-laden with wool, grain, frozen meat, timber, metals and manufactured goods.

In and about Sydney are more indications of what is considered to be the Australian way of life than in any other city. Look out over the harbour on any summer weekend and you will see the water dappled with sails; go to a beach (there are enough of them to visit a different one each week) and you will meet huge crowds—tanned, athletic, casually dressed, fun-loving, gregarious, yet independent.

Around Sydney Cove, where the original settlement was established, the most modern of multi-storied buildings are mushrooming up against the ever-changing skyline. Here also, at the eastern end of the cove and overlooking the harbour, is the £16,000,000 Sydney Opera House—as modern as tomorrow. But Government House, only a stone's throw away, is reminiscent of an English castle.

Contrasts are at one's elbow everywhere in Sydney. From the spacious baronial homes of its most successful business-men to attic flats in crowded, cosmopolitan, wonderful Kings Cross—from the tranquillity of its harbour bays to the roar of the ceaseless traffic crossing its gigantic steel bridge, this is a fabulous city.

SYDNEY residents are lucky in having some magnificent sheltered waterways, as well as the open sea, on their doorstep. For those who live—in the southern suburbs there is Botany Bay, and a little farther on Port Hacking; for the centrally situated, the Harbour itself (Port Jackson) with North Harbour and Middle Harbour running off it; and those of the northern suburbs have the incomparable reaches of Pittwater, Cowan Creek, and Coal and Candle Creek beckoning to them over their back fences, for these are part of the extensive Hawkesbury River–Broken Bay system.

Navigable waterways such as these, in natural bushland settings of great beauty, have helped to make Australians one of the most boat-conscious people in the world, be it yachts or power-boats that appeal to them. Look at this picture of Bobbin Head, near the head of Cowan Creek, and you will see why.

PLATE 48
Bobbin Head, New South Wales.

IT WAS not until 1813, that a route was found through the Blue Mountains west of Sydney; until then this range had hampered the development of New South Wales by forming an impenetrable barrier to the vast fertile grazing lands beyond. Two years after the route was discovered, a road was put through, opening up the inland to exploration and exploitation. Now there is an arterial highway and a network of roads and tracks linking up all the townships and scenic features of this area. Only about thirty-five miles from Sydney, but 3,500 feet above sea-level, it is the city's favourite mountain resort.

The Blue Mountains are a heavily indented spur of the Great Dividing Range. Their sheer-sided, castellated walls of ochre and sienna-coloured sandstone thrust aggressively into the densely forested valleys. The mountains derive their name from the almost incredibly hazy blue which Sir Arthur Streeton, Elioth Gruner and other Australian artists have so successfully transferred to their canvases.

The triassic sandstone formation shown here, known as the Three Sisters, rises 1,000 feet almost vertically from the floor of the Jamieson Valley; it is one of the outstanding attractions of the Blue Mountains area. Striking at any time, it is best seen when the lowering sun enhances the warm tones of the rock, setting them in yet greater contrast to the blue distance beyond and below.

PLATE 49
Three Sisters, Blue Mountains, New South Wales.

AUSTRALIANS are fortunate in having many roads and highways which follow the perimeter of their continent, for along these the sea, with all its attractions, is never far away. The Cook Highway, north of Cairns, traces an idyllic shore of sparkling sapphire-blue ocean, with truly golden sands backed by tropical palms and the mountains in their unending green jungle; the Great Ocean Road of Victoria follows the rugged contours of the coast with plenty of safe bathing and surfing beaches in between, to name only two.

New South Wales is perhaps the best endowed of all in this respect, for the entire eastern seaboard is a succession of sandy beaches between high, rocky headlands. Along this coast the pounding of heavy surf adds its unmistakable signature, thrilling to those who delight in riding boards on its high crests.

Something of the dramatic face of Australia's coasts is shown in this view from Stanwell Park, about forty miles south of Sydney.

PLATE 50
Stanwell Park, New South Wales.

A TREMENDOUS engineering project, the biggest ever under-taken in Australia, is being carried out in southern New South Wales and northern Victoria. This is the Snowy Mountains Scheme, a combined irrigation and hydro-electric power-generation system which will eventually cost about £400,000,000.

In the heart of the Australian Alps, the waters of the Snowy River and its tributary, the Eucumbene, are being turned back through the mountains, away from their normal course through well-watered country in south-eastern Victoria, where they are not needed. Instead, they are being diverted to augment the flow of the Murray and Murrumbidgee Rivers by about 2,000,000 acre-feet each year, for use in their dry but fertile valleys. More irrigation in these valleys will increase the value of annual production there by approximately £30,000,000.

Before being released for this purpose, the water will have passed through some of the series of tunnels totalling eighty-five miles; it will have been held in one or more of the seven major and twelve smaller dams; and it will have produced electricity in fifteen power-stations. The power output should ensure the peak-load requirements of Victoria and New South Wales for several years to come.

The Snowy Mountains are the subject of this picture, taken on the road leading down to one of the power-stations, Tumut No. 1, where 320,000 kilowatts are produced 1,000 feet below the surface.

PLATE 51
Snowy Mountains, New South Wales.

CANBERRA, the capital of the Commonwealth of Australia, grew out of controversy. Following Federation in 1901, there was animosity between the States about the site of the Federal capital; a separate and independent place on Australian Commonwealth Territory was decided upon in 1908, but it was not until 1927 that the Federal Parliament sat in the long, low white building shown in this photograph.

Since those days, a vast change has come over the face of Canberra. The isolated buildings, surrounded by sheep pastures in a broad shallow valley, have given way to an idyllic city of fine, modern buildings, reflecting the designs of architects of vision. It is laid out geometrically, in circles, hexagonals, oblongs and ellipses. In the parks and reserves, along the boulevards, in private gardens—everywhere, in fact—there are trees. In spring, the whole place is fragrant with blossom, and in autumn the pin-oaks, poplars, birches, copper beeches, elms and other deciduous trees make it as colourful as any New England fall. There are gum trees too, in their thousands, and the bush itself is not far away.

This is a clean and spacious city, without slums or the necessity of heavy industries. The increasing tempo of building is in homes, schools, research establishments, and features of beauty, such as a great lake dividing the two main sections of the town.

In Canberra's newly completed City Square is an appropriate statue—Ethos, "the spirit of the community". Australians may well be confident that their capital, now and in the future, will be a true symbol of Federation and their way of life.

PLATE 52
Canberra, Australian Capital Territory.

FRONT COVER
Mount Beerwah, Glasshouse Mountains, Queensland.

THE bold, high wedge of Mount Beerwah, in the Glasshouse Mountains district of Queensland, is an arresting sight from any angle, but most of all when it is seen shawled in the blue of distance, against the fresh greens of its surrounding forests and the red volcanic soil.

Trees are an essential part of the Australian scene. The blue-gums and white-gums, casuarinas, tea-trees and stringy-barks in the forest illustrated here contribute strongly to this landscape, and the road invites you to travel on and see more of Australia in the pages of this book.

BACK COVER
Mount Warning, New South Wales.

ALONG the south arm of the Tweed River, in northern New South Wales, there are many beautiful and moody landscapes. Most are dominated by the 3,800-foot peak of Mount Warning, which rises head and shoulders above the hilly countryside. It was named by Captain Cook in 1770, to remind sailors to beware of the Fingal Head rocks, close to Tweed Heads, on what is now the Queensland-New South Wales border.

The rain-forest in this area, with its variety and luxuriance, is virtually jungle, but much of the forest has been cleared to make way for dairy farms and banana plantations.

FRONTISPIECE
Russell Falls, Tasmania.

ALTHOUGH there are many bigger waterfalls in Australia, none can compete in beauty with the Russell Falls in Tasmania.

They lie within fifty miles of Hobart, at the end of a good road which follows the wide and sleepy Derwent River to New Norfolk, then wanders between the poplar-girt hopfields and oast-houses of Bushy, and through a great forest of eucalypts.